Key Skills Level 1:
Communication

Written to the 2004 Standards

Roslyn Whitley Willis

Series Editor

Roslyn Whitley Willis

**Published by
Lexden Publishing Ltd
www.lexden-publishing.co.uk**

To ensure that your book is up to date visit:
www.lexden-publishing.co.uk/keyskills/update.htm

Acknowledgements

Thanks go to my husband for his contribution in naming some of the fictitious organisations that, and people who, appear in this book, together with his forbearance and encouragement. Special thanks go to Jean Coates just for being there for me, and believing in me,
as ever – *Roslyn Whitley Willis*..

I would like to thank the publisher, Mark Kench, whose belief and hard work helped the project reach fruition.

First Published in 2007 by Lexden Publishing Ltd.

Cover photograph of juggling balls by kind permission of Marcel Hol ©

British Library Cataloguing in Publication Data.

A CIP record of this book is available from the British Library.

ISBN: 978-1-904995-30-2

Typeset and designed by Lexden Publishing Ltd

Printed by Lightning Source.

Lexden Publishing Ltd
23 Irvine Road
Colchester
Essex CO3 3TS

Telephone: 01206 533164
Email: info@lexden-publishing.co.uk
www.lexden-publishing.co.uk

PREFACE

The material in this book gives you the opportunity to understand Key Skills and practise them so you are able to meet the high standards set out in the Level 1 Key Skills Standards for Application of Number.

The introductory section of this book explains each of the Key Skills and how to gain a qualification.

This book is further divided into three distinct parts:

1   Reference Sheets

This section provides all the necessary background information to prepare you for Level 2 Application of Number. It provides useful exercises that will:

     aid your learning;

     can be used for revision; and

     prepare and aid you for the Part A Tasks and End Assessment questions.

2   Part A Practice Tasks

Working through these will help you produce work at the right level and prepare you for the End Assessment.

As you complete each task you will become more confident about what is expected in Key Skills and be able to use your knowledge and understanding to pass the End Assessment and put together a Portfolio of Evidence.

3   End Assessment Questions

This section provides examples of the type of questions that are likely to appear on an End Assessment paper and that you may have to pass as part of your Key Skills qualification.

Further resources

When your tutor thinks you have enough knowledge of Key Skills, she/he will give you an assignment, or assignments, to complete. Working successfully through the assignment(s) will show you are able to apply your knowledge and understanding, and produce work that will go into your Key Skills Portfolio of Evidence. These assignments are contained in the *Tutor's Resource* cd.

Additional resources and information can be found at www.lexden-publishing.co.uk/keyskills.

WHAT ARE KEY SKILLS? – A STUDENT'S GUIDE

Key Skills are important for everything you do, at school, at college, at work and at home. They will help you in your vocational studies and prepare you for the skills you will use in education and training and the work you will do in the future.

Key Skills are at the centre of your learning, and the work in this book provides you with the opportunity to develop and practise the Key Skills of Communication, Application of Number and Information and Communication Technology, through a variety of tasks. Having Key Skills knowledge will help you apply them to other areas of your studies.

There are six Key Skills

Communication is about writing and speaking.	**Application of Number** is about numbers.	**Information and Communication Technology** is about communicating using IT.
It will help you develop your skills in: • speaking; • listening; • researching; • reading; • writing; • presenting information in the form of text and images, including diagrams, charts and graphs.	It will help you develop your skills in: • collecting information; • carrying out calculations; • understanding the results of your calculations; • presenting your findings in a variety of ways, such as graphs and diagrams.	It will help you develop your skills in using computers to: • find and store information; • produce information using text and images and numbers; • develop your presentation of documents; • communicate information to other people.
Improving Own Learning and Performance is about planning and reviewing your work.	**Problem Solving** is about understanding and solving problems.	**Working with Others** is about working effectively with other people and giving support to them.
It will help you develop your skills in: • setting targets; • setting deadlines; • following your action plan of targets and deadlines; • reviewing your progress; • reviewing your achievements; • identifying your strengths and weaknesses.	It will help you develop your skills in: • identifying the problem; • coming up with solutions to the problem; • selecting ways of tackling the problem; • planning what you need to do to solve the problem; • following your plan; • deciding if you have solved the problem; • reviewing your problem solving techniques.	It will help you develop your skills in: • working with another, or several, person(s); • deciding on the roles and responsibilities of each person; • putting together an action plan of targets and responsibilities; • carrying out your responsibilities; • supporting other members of the group; • reviewing progress; • reviewing your achievements; • identifying the strengths and weaknesses of working with other people.

HOW TO GAIN A KEY SKILLS QUALIFICATION

Mandatory Key Skills

Communication
Application of Number
ICT

Practise Part A Key Skills tasks in this book to help you:

Put together a **Portfolio of Evidence**

Usually an assignment written for you by your tutor to cover the Key Skill, or a number of Key Skills in one piece of work.

The Portfolio is based on Part B of the Key Skill Standards.

Pass a test – called an **End Assessment**

This test is 40 multiple-choice questions and, at Levels 1 and 2, you have either 1 hour or 1 hour 15 minutes to complete it depending on the Key Skill.

The questions are based on Part A of the Key Skill Standards.

Good News!

If you already have some GCSE or ICT qualifications, it may not be necessary for you to take the End Assessment! Your tutor will help you with this – it is called **PROXY QUALIFICATIONS.**

Wider Key Skills

Improving Own Learning and Performance
Problem Solving
Working with Others

Practise Part A Key Skills tasks in your vocational studies to help you:

Put together a **Portfolio of Evidence**

Usually included in an assignment written for you by your tutor to cover the Key Skills of Communication, Application of Number or ICT.

The Portfolio is based on Part B of the Key Skill Standards.

Opportunities to work towards achieving the Wider Key Skills are provided in the Portfolio assignment work and are included in the *Tutor's Resource* that accompanies this text.

THE PORTFOLIO

STEP 1

Once your tutor has assessed your assignment work and you have passed, you will put your work into your portfolio.

A **Portfolio of Evidence** usually takes the form of a lever arch file with a **Portfolio Front Sheet** that shows:

 where you are studying;

 which course you are studying;

 which Key Skill(s) are in the portfolio;

 when you passed your End Assessment(s); and

 details of any Proxy Qualifications.

STEP 2

It is important to number every page of the work you put in your portfolio. This helps you complete the **Log Book** that your tutor will give you.

STEP 3

Complete the Log Book. This indicates where your evidence is to be found and also describes what is in the portfolio.

STEP 4

Check your Log Book entries carefully, making sure everything is correct and neat.

Get your tutor to check you have put your Portfolio together correctly.

STEP 5

Sign the Log Book and get the person who assessed your work to sign too.

Once you have completed your Portfolio of Evidence it is shown to someone outside your centre whose job it is to check it meets the Key Skills Standards. If this person agrees that it does, then you have **passed your Portfolio of Evidence**.

Chapter 1: Communication

At **Level 1**, learners need to use the skills of speaking, listening, reading and writing in straightforward tasks. You will be able to identify the main points in reading material and in discussions.

Additionally you will have to show you can take part in discussions about everyday subjects.

When reading material, you will be able to identify the main points and ideas and you will be able to write short documents using simple language and, sometimes, appropriate images to emphasise the meaning.

Correct spelling, grammar and punctuation are important.

The following reference sheets provide opportunities for you to review and practise the communication skills needed for Key Skills.

COMPLETING FORMS AND JOB APPLICATION FORMS

When completing forms of any type, be it a form to open a bank account, or a mobile phone account, a student rail card, a passport, a holiday or a job application form, **accuracy** and **neatness** are vitally important.

Before you put pen to paper do the following:

- Study the form, all its questions and sections, so you know what information you will be expected to provide.

- If possible, photocopy the form, and practise filling it in. This will help you judge how large or small your writing should be in order to add the information required. It also shows you what your completed form will look like and help you decide if you can improve how you express your information and present your form.

- Carry out any research you need for the questions asked. For instance, you may have to provide information that you have stored somewhere; studying the form's questions alerts you to the fact that you need to **find that information**.

When completing the form do the following:

- Use **BLACK INK** and **BLOCK CAPITALS** – these guidelines are usually stated on the form and you will be aware of them having read it carefully and thoroughly before completing it.

- Use neat handwriting that is easy to read.

- Fill in every section – even if it means putting **Not Applicable** in some sections.

- Make sure you answer each question fully.

- Make sure you have deleted inapplicable information (usually indicated by an asterisk (*)) on the form, for instance *delete whichever is not applicable.*

- Check your spelling is correct.

- Be honest.

- Keep a copy of the form before you send it off.

You will have to complete a variety of forms throughout your life. These simple guidelines will make that process easier and you will be confident of getting it right and portraying the right image.

Job application forms

The tips on above apply equally to **job application forms**, but there are some extra points to consider.

Namely:

- Research the company carefully. You will probably be asked a question at interview that will check how much you know about the company, its product(s), partners, etc., etc., and your research is vital.

- Read the job description carefully so you can be clear about what skills and qualities the employer sees as important. You can then make sure you include information on your application form to support the fact that you have some of these qualities and skills.

- Include details of qualifications you have achieved (don't include failures, your application form must concentrate on **positive** aspects).

Confirm, before naming them, who your referees are to be. It is bad manners to quote someone's name as willing to give you a reference if you have not received their permission in the first place. They may refuse to act as referee if you do not clear it with them first.

Be sure to include a **job reference number** if one was quoted in the advertisement.

Use sentences rather than just bullet points throughout the form.

Check, and double check, spelling, grammar and punctuation.

Sound positive and enthusiastic.

Do not lie.

Take a copy of the form to refer to **before** the interview. You will probably apply for several jobs at the same time and you will need to remember what you said to each prospective employer.

Return the form **well before the closing date**, and make sure you keep the form **clean, tidy and as uncrumpled** as possible.

The purpose of your neatly, accurately completed job application form

A prospective employer, on reading your form should have a positive idea of the following:

How your personality and qualities are suited to the job and the company.

How your qualifications and skills are suited to the job and the company.

How you have given your application careful consideration.

USING IMAGES IN COMMUNICATION

Images can be used to enhance and explain written communications.

Remember, use images to **enhance the text**, and to help the reader's understanding of the text. An image may also provide information in addition to text. **An image should not be included if it has no relevance**.

Think carefully about why you are using images and only use appropriate images in appropriate places.

Presenting numerical data in visual form

There are a number of situations when you will find it necessary, or preferable, to produce visual representations of numbers. Some people find it easier to understand figures when presented in graphical form, rather than table form. By all means consider using both a table and a graph, thus providing a number of ways in which the reader can understand the information.

Data in tabular form

INTERNATIONAL TEMPERATURES		
3rd January 2006		
CITY	MIN	MAX
Lisbon	10	14
Madrid	-2	12
London	3	12
Brussels	6	10
Amsterdam	6	8
Helsinki	1	2

Data in graphical form

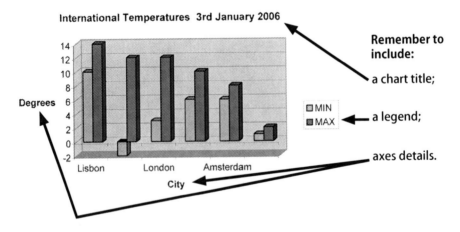

The purpose of including the chart and the table is to allow the reader to understand and interpret the information in the most suitable way.

CRUISING ON THE AIDAblu
– a P&O* Cruise Liner

Imagine... it's 7.30 am and the sun is just beginning to rise above the mountains that run down to the sea... you've had breakfast in one of the four restaurants... you are on deck watching the beautiful island of Madeira get closer as your floating, luxury hotel edges slowly into port... the forecast for the day ahead is 28°... you've all day to explore today's destination and will probably have dinner in one of the restaurants as AIDAblu leaves port at 8 pm.

Come and experience the relaxing life on board our latest cruise liner

The AIDAblu entering the port of Funchal, Madeira

We'll include visits to some of the most beautiful islands and ports in the Atlantic

A member of Dubai Ports World

The inclusion of an image in this article helps the reader to identify the 'product' that is being discussed and adds interest to facts and figures.

In this instance, the *text* is being used to aid the readers' understanding of the images.

WEATHER UK
20th February 2006

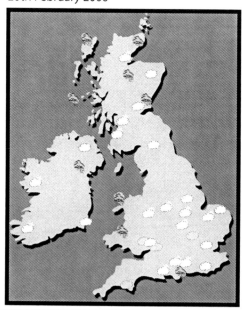

WEATHER UK
20th February 2006

Norfolk and Suffolk

There are few clouds at 2000 feet

Visibility is 7000m

Cornwall and Devon

Light rain at 1300 feet

Broken rain clouds at 1600 feet

Wind speed 18-36 mph

USING THE TELEPHONE AND MAKING TELEPHONE CALLS

Before you place a call

- Think about what you wish to say and how you will say it. Courtesy is expected when using the telephone just as if you are talking in person.

- Make a list of what you need to say and the information you need to give and/or receive **before placing the call. BE PREPARED.**

- Dialling too quickly may be the cause of dialling a wrong number, never just hang up. Apologise and let the person who answered the telephone know you have dialled the incorrect number.

How to speak on the telephone

- When speaking, think of the way you sound. On the telephone sounds and moods are magnified. **Talk with a smile in your voice**. The person on the other end of the telephone cannot see your facial expressions and your tone of voice will need to express politeness, enthusiasm and efficiency.

- Make sure you say your words clearly and precisely. It is embarrassing, and time-wasting, to be asked to repeat what you are saying.

Making telephone calls

- It is polite, and necessary, to identify yourself. If you are calling from a company, then you would need to identify your company, your name, and perhaps your department, before going on to say why you are calling. For instance:

  Good morning, this is Blackwood and Company of York. Janet speaking from the Purchasing Department. I am ringing to place an order...... I wish to speak to ....

How to answer a ringing telephone

- The proper way to answer the telephone is give a greeting – **hello; good afternoon** – followed by identifying your telephone number if it is your home, or your name and your company. **Never** answer with just "hello" or "yes". Hello is useless because it does not tell the caller anything, and "yes" is curt and impolite, and again it does not tell the caller anything – except perhaps that you are in a bad mood and cannot be bothered.

Good manners on the telephone

- Answer a ringing telephone promptly.

- If you dial a number that is wrong, apologise promptly and hang up.

- Calling a business at or very near closing time is thoughtless and not likely to result in a successful call.

- Introduce yourself when placing a call.

- Answer a phone by identifying yourself, your company and/or your department.

- When speaking to anyone who is working and for whom time is important, make your call informative and short – plan ahead.

- It is polite to let the person who **made** the call **end** the call.

SENDING FAXES

Facsimile transmission

A fax is an efficient, and speedy, method of communication and can be used to send text and images. However, there are some important points to consider when sending a fax.

When and what to fax

Always make sure the message is clear and take into account the following:

- Only send faxes when communication is **URGENT** – email would be another suitable method of urgently communicating something, but a fax can be used when someone does not have email, but does have a fax machine.

- **Don't count on privacy** – remember that it is not always the case that the person to whom the fax is being sent has their own fax machine. Most companies have centrally-placed fax machines. For this reason be aware that the message can be seen and read by anyone. Do not send sensitive or confidential information in this way.

Always use a **Fax Cover Sheet**. It should contain the following information:

- The receiver's name and fax number.

- Your name, your business name, address, telephone number, fax number.

- The date (and possibly time).

- The total number of pages being transmitted, including the cover sheet. When you list the number of pages, it means the recipient can check that all pages have been received.

- A list of what you are faxing to ensure that the other party receives everything you've faxed.

- Cover sheets may also include special notations, such as "Urgent" and "For Immediate Delivery".

Some things do not fax well

- Limit the use of dark colours as they increase transmission time and use the recipient's ink!

- Do not use light colours for text as they may not be seen by the fax machine as dark enough to register.

- Try to avoid colour images and photographs in faxes.

Fax cover sheet

Clearly mark who the fax is **to**. (If the company to which you are sending the fax has a centrally-placed fax machine, make sure the fax gets to the right person by clearly identifying the recipient's name and job title.)

Include the **fax number**. (If your company has a central fax machine, it may not be you who sends the fax, but a telephonist. Make sure she/he can see the fax number clearly.)

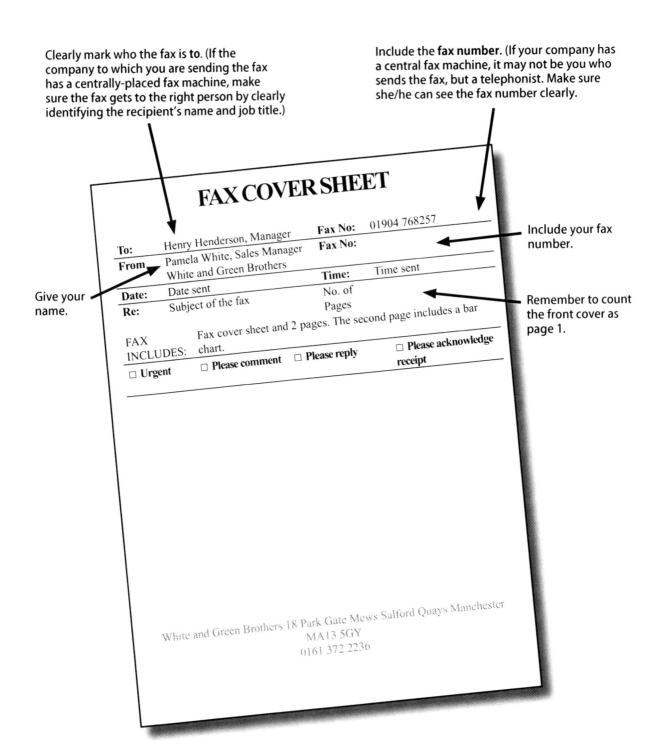

FAX COVER SHEET

To:	Henry Henderson, Manager	**Fax No:**	01904 768257
From	Pamela White, Sales Manager	**Fax No:**	
	White and Green Brothers	**Time:**	Time sent
Date:	Date sent	No. of	
Re:	Subject of the fax	Pages	

FAX INCLUDES: Fax cover sheet and 2 pages. The second page includes a bar chart.

☐ Urgent   ☐ **Please comment**   ☐ **Please reply**   ☐ **Please acknowledge receipt**

White and Green Brothers 18 Park Gate Mews Salford Quays Manchester
MA13 5GY
0161 372 2236

Include your fax number.

Give your name.

Remember to count the front cover as page 1.

WRITING AND SETTING OUT PERSONAL LETTERS

A personal letter is a letter written from someone's home address to either:

 a company – for instance to accompany a job application, or to complain about something; or

 a friend – for instance to invite a friend to stay with you.

Some points to remember about letter writing

 Firstly: the date.

Put the date the letter is written. This date should be shown as:

dd/mm/yyyy

that is: 14th June 2007. Don't mix this order.

 Secondly: the name and address to where the letter is being sent.

Remember to write to a **person** if you can;

that is: Mr Jaz Allahan.

If you don't know the name of the person, address the letter to a job title;

that is: The Marketing Manager.

> **REMEMBER**
>
> **Don't just write Allahan and Corby Ltd. A COMPANY cannot open a letter, but a PERSON can!**

 Thirdly: who are you writing to?

When you write "Dear ...." it is called the **salutation**.

When you write "Yours ...." it is called the **complimentary close**.

The salutation and complimentary close must match.

That is: Dear Mr Jones = Yours sincerely

Dear Sirs = Yours faithfully

When you use a person's name, be sincere!

> **Note**
>
> **Only the word *Yours* has a capital letter at the beginning.**

 Fourthly: sign the letter.

A letter from you needs to be signed. After the complimentary close, leave yourself space for a signature, then print your name. This is important because your signature may not be readable and the person who receives the letter will not know your name.

Examples of address, salutation and complimentary close

Name and address:	Mr P Marks Sunningbrow Golf Course Sunningbrow Hill Aberdeen AB7 3NH
Salutation:	Dear Mr Marks
	Never write Dear Mr P Marks – just Dear Mr Marks. Think of how you would address him if meeting him. You would say "Mr Marks", so write it as you would say it.
Complimentary close:	Yours sincerely
	You have used his name, so be SINCERE!

Name and address:	The Sales Manager McKie and Aston plc 8 School Fields York YO14 5ND
Salutation:	Dear Sir or Madam
	because you have not used a name
Complimentary close:	Yours faithfully
	You have not used a name, so how can you be SINCERE!

Name and address:	Mrs K Trent Office Manager T&N Agency Villamoura Road Bexhill on Sea Sussex SX5 7BQ **This time you have used a name and a job title.**
Salutation:	Dear Mrs Trent
	because you have addressed the letter to her
Complimentary close:	Yours sincerely
	You have used her name, so be SINCERE!

A personal letter written to a company

The following is an example of a personal letter written to a company:

Writer's home address, or return address. Don't put your name here.

The address and telephone number/email address can be:

- in the centre;
- at the right hand side;
- at the left hand side; or
- a combination as seen in this example.

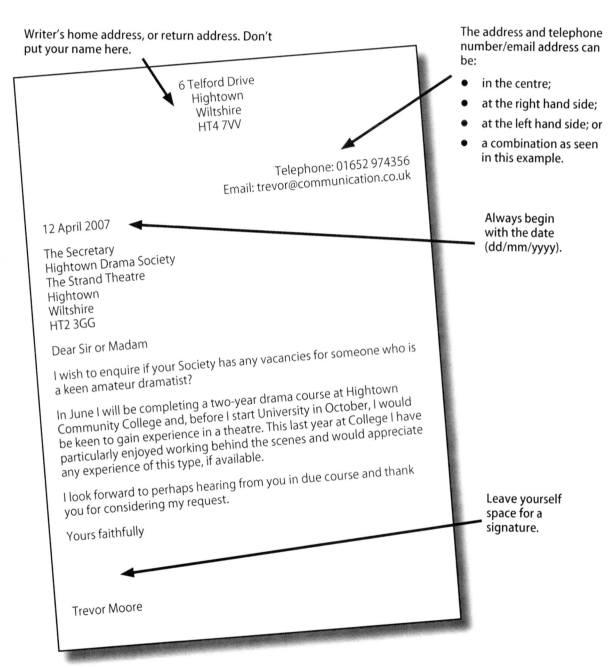

6 Telford Drive
Hightown
Wiltshire
HT4 7VV

Telephone: 01652 974356
Email: trevor@communication.co.uk

Always begin with the date (dd/mm/yyyy).

12 April 2007

The Secretary
Hightown Drama Society
The Strand Theatre
Hightown
Wiltshire
HT2 3GG

Dear Sir or Madam

I wish to enquire if your Society has any vacancies for someone who is a keen amateur dramatist?

In June I will be completing a two-year drama course at Hightown Community College and, before I start University in October, I would be keen to gain experience in a theatre. This last year at College I have particularly enjoyed working behind the scenes and would appreciate any experience of this type, if available.

I look forward to perhaps hearing from you in due course and thank you for considering my request.

Yours faithfully

Leave yourself space for a signature.

Trevor Moore

The letter is addressed to someone's title because the name of the recipient is unknown.
In this way the **salutation** is Dear Sir or Madam
The **complimentary close** is Yours faithfully

Note: It is usual for a female to write her title: Mrs Tina Moore or Tina Moore (Mrs)
A MAN NEVER CALLS HIMSELF MR. So if you receive a letter from 'T Moore', you can assume it is from a man!

WRITING AND SETTING OUT BUSINESS LETTERS

A business letter is an **external** method of communication and reflects how an organisation communicates with, and is viewed by, people and organisations outside the business.

There are a number of purposes for business letters:

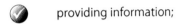 providing information;

giving instructions;

confirming arrangements;

improving customer services;

public relations.

A business letter has three parts:

1   introductory paragraph;

2   middle paragraph(s);

3   closing paragraph.

Introductory paragraph

The introduction/opening paragraph introduces the theme/purpose of the letter and puts it into a context or background.

Introductory paragraphs are also used to mention essential people, events or things to which the letter will refer.

Middle paragraph(s)

These provide detailed information.

The middle paragraphs of a letter **develop a theme** and **provide all relevant details** and particulars. The number of paragraphs used will depend upon the complexity of the letter's subject. However, paragraphs should be kept fairly short and deal with only one topic at a time. **New topic = new paragraph** is something you must keep in mind.

Closing paragraph

This provides an action statement and a courteous close.

In this paragraph you will attempt to summarise your comments and state what action you will take, or wish to be taken.

Some letters are concluded with a courteous sentence to act as a means of signalling the end of the document.

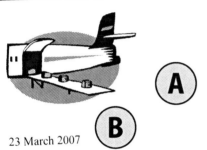

WITH CARE
AIR CARGO HANDLING PLC

Hanger 18R, Manchester Airport, Manchester MR4 6JE
0161 346 98667
email: **withcare@manair.aviation.com**

23 March 2007

Mr Peter Phillips
Despatch Department Manager
Mercury Components plc
Unit 7
Coniston Industrial Park
BARNSLEY
South Yorkshire
SO13 6BN

Dear Mr Phillips

AIR FREIGHT TO CHICAGO 4 April 2007

Thank you for your company's recent request to quote for transporting a packing crate to Chicago.

As you know, our Mike Richards came to your organisation yesterday to examine the crate, take its measurements and establish its weight. As a result of his visit we are pleased to be able to quote the sum of £568.90 + VAT. Our formal quotation is enclosed with this letter.

For this sum we will:

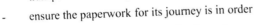

- collect the crate on 2 April before 12 noon
- transport it to our depot at Manchester Airport
- ensure the paperwork for its journey is in order
- obtain UK Customs clearance for the crate
- put it on flight WC457 departing at 1520 hours on 4 April, for Chicago O'Hare Airport
- upon arrival, arrange for our American handlers to unload the crate and obtain US Customs clearance
- store safely in the depot until your US client

We trust this quotation is acceptable and look forward to assisting you on this occasion. We would need confirmation of your wish to employ our services no later than 28 March.

If you wish to discuss this matter further, please do not hesitate to contact me.

My direct line number is 0161 346 2323.

Yours sincerely

Paul Falcon
Procurement Manager
Enc

Key to parts of a business letter

(A) The **letter heading** of the company including a company logo.

(B) **Date** expressed as dd/mm/yyyy.

(C) **Name**, **title** and **company name** and **address** of the person and company receiving the letter.

(D) **Salutation** – Dear Mr Phillips because the letter is addressed to him in the name and address line.

(E) **Heading**: indicating what the letter is about.

(F) **Introductory paragraph**.

(G) **Middle paragraphs** providing details.

(H) **Closing paragraphs** providing an action statement and a courteous close.

(I) **Complimentary close**: Yours sincerely because the recipient's name is used in the salutation. The writer's name and title, leaving space for his signature!

(J) **Enc** indicating there is an enclosure.

Useful phrases for business letters

Thank you for your letter dated ....

As you may know ....

I wish to inform you that ....

I was pleased to hear that ....

I wish to enquire about ....

I should like to place an order for ....

I look forward to hearing from you in the near future.

I should be grateful if you would kindly send me ....

Following our recent telephone conversation, I wish to ....

Please do not hesitate to let me know if I can do anything further to help ....

WRITING AND SETTING OUT MEMOS

A memorandum – plural memoranda
(abbreviated to memo)

A memo is an **internal** method of communication.

Memos must be short documents, and usually deal with one subject. A long document within an organisation is usually sent in the form of a report.

The memo should be signed by the sender.

Although organisations have their own style of layout for memos, all memos contain these essential headings:

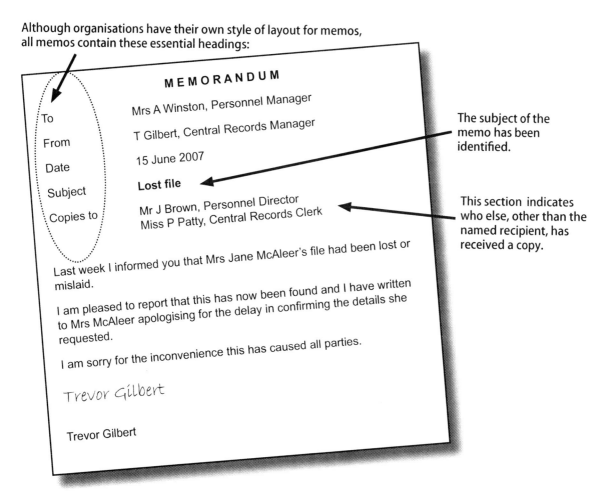

MEMORANDUM

To

From

Date

Subject

Copies to

Mrs A Winston, Personnel Manager

T Gilbert, Central Records Manager

15 June 2007

Lost file

Mr J Brown, Personnel Director
Miss P Patty, Central Records Clerk

The subject of the memo has been identified.

This section indicates who else, other than the named recipient, has received a copy.

Last week I informed you that Mrs Jane McAleer's file had been lost or mislaid.

I am pleased to report that this has now been found and I have written to Mrs McAleer apologising for the delay in confirming the details she requested.

I am sorry for the inconvenience this has caused all parties.

Trevor Gilbert

Trevor Gilbert

Typical layout of a memorandum (memo). This is formal as it includes their titles (Mr, Mrs, Personnel Manager, etc.).

In this example you will see the message is short and simple and deals with only one point.

Who the memo is from, and to whom it is being sent, are identified and the document is dated and signed.

Informal memo

This is an example of an **informal** memo:

MEMORANDUM

To   Janet Markham, Advertising Department

From   Catherine Woodleigh, Purchasing Department

Date   15 June 2007

Re   Company's Sales Brochure

The 2,000 copies of the company's Christmas brochure have been received from the printer today.

These are available for you to collect at your earliest convenience.

Catherine

In this example, the names have no title and there are no company titles included – although people's departments are shown. This is important because an organisation could employ people with the same name but who work in different departments.

The memo is dated. There is a subject – this time expressed as 're' (short for 'reference').

The memo is signed with the sender's first name only – the surname could be included.

TAKING MESSAGES

It is always helpful to use a standard message form to record a message, whether it is a telephone message or a message of another kind. The headings on a standard form will help you include the information needed.

There is a message form on *page 22*, but this is not the only layout that companies use.

Remember you should always:

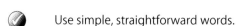 Use simple, straightforward words.

Keep your sentences short but vary the length a little so that the message reads well.

Include **all, and only, the key facts and information.**

Leave out irrelevant information.

If you are repeating a request for the reader of the message to **do something**, make it a request **not an order**.

Be very specific and clear about days, dates and times. If you have to give a non-specific time, e.g. "tomorrow", add the day and date in case your message is not read immediately. It is advisable to always be specific about days and dates in order to avoid confusion.

Mark urgent messages clearly.

Your responsibility does not end when you place the message on the right desk – it only ends when the person has read it and understood it.

Identifying the key facts

Every message contains key facts. If you miss them out of the message it will not make sense – or not make **complete sense**.

Business callers are normally quite good at giving the key facts in an ordered way and checking them through afterwards. Private callers may be less helpful and some may like to chat, so that it becomes difficult to sort out what is important from what is not.

A good way to check you have the message clear in your mind is to read back your summary to the caller. This both checks that you have the message correctly with all the important facts, and gives the caller the opportunity to alter or add anything.

MESSAGE FORM

TO..DEPARTMENT...

DATE ....TIME ....

CALLER'S NAME...

ORGANISATION ....

TELEPHONE NUMBER...FAX NUMBER...

EMAIL ADDRESS ....

✓ Appropriate box(es)

Telephoned	☐
Returned your call	☐
Called to see you	☐
Left a message	☐
Requests you call back	☐
Please arrange an appointment	☐

Message

....

....

....

....

....

....

....

Taken by .... Department... Time............................

WRITING REPORTS

In common with any other business document, a report needs to be planned and, before beginning, you must consider the following:

 A report will usually be requested by people who need the information for a specific purpose.

 A report differs from an essay in that it is designed to provide information that will be acted on, rather than to be read by people interested in the ideas for their own sake. Because of this, it has a different structure and layout.

 Do not write in the first person.

 Use the past tense to describe your findings.

"It was found that......... etc., etc". **It** rather than **I** and the past tense of the verb to find, i.e. **found**.

Points to consider before beginning your report

For whom am I writing the report?

A named individual, or a group of people?

Person(s) who have no knowledge of the subject matter?

What do the readers need to know?

What do the readers already know?

What is my objective?

To inform the readers?

To explain ideas?

To persuade?

To transmit ideas or information, facts or findings?

What is the context?

Urgent/important?

Routine?

If you skip the planning stage, poor preparation invariably causes time-consuming problems at a later stage.

Example of a report's title page and content

A Report

For

The Village Council

on

The possibility of holding monthly Farmers' Markets in the Village Square

Written by

Niamh Connelly

7 April 2007

FINDINGS

This report was requested by the Village Council in order that it could decide whether to agree to hold a monthly Farmers' Market in the Village Square.

In order to produce this report it was necessary to conduct research into the following topics:

- Farmers and suppliers interested in the scheme*
- Village residents interested in attending the markets*

1 Farmers and suppliers interested in participating in the scheme.

Make an opening statement about the topic and its relevance to the Report then separate into sub-headings, which may, or may not, be numbered.

1.1   Farmers from this county

1.2   Farmers from neighbouring counties

1.3   Cheese makers

1.4   etc., etc.

2   Village residents who expressed an interest in attending the proposed markets.

RECOMMENDATIONS AND REASONS FOR THE RECOMMENDATIONS
(Describe your findings)

As a result of the research undertaken (outlined in Appendix 4), the writer recommends the Village Council consider introducing Farmers' Markets for a period of six months, after which time a review is recommended.

Describe the recommendations, making use of paragraphs, headings, bullet points, underlined headings, emboldened text, etc.

Sign the Report

Date the Report

> *** Note:** These are the topics you have researched and which you will explain in detail in separate paragraphs.

Structuring a report

A report is used for reference and is often quite a lengthy document. It has to be clearly structured for you and your readers to quickly find the information wanted.

Parts of a report

The nature of the report will vary from routine reports to complex, non-routine reports. The layout will vary too, yet all reports should have the following common features:

Cover sheet

This should contain the following:

  full title of the report;

  your name;

  the name of the person(s) for whom the report is intended;

  the date.

You need to know this information before you begin the process of producing the report:

  what?

  why?

  who?

Main sections/findings

The report will need to be divided into various logical sections and sub-sections. Make full use of **paragraph headings** and **paragraph numbering** including **bullet points**.

This is the section in which you:

  state what you found out;

  clearly present your results, making use of paragraphs, paragraph headings, bullet points, etc.;

  list the essential data. You may want to use tables, graphs and figures.

Use a consistent system of display throughout. Numbered paragraphs might be 1, 2, 3, or 1.1, 1.2, 1.3, etc.

Using effective "signposting" in this way will help the reader pick out elements of the report and will ensure the whole document is easy to follow.

Recommendations

Any recommendations you make must be presented clearly and follow logically from the conclusions.

This section might, for example, suggest a preferred option from several that were under consideration, make new proposals or recommend further research or investigation.

WRITING A CV (CURRICULUM VITAE)

A CV (Curriculum Vitae) is a document that gives a brief account of someone's:

 education;

 qualifications; and

 experience;

and is written by a job applicant to give information to a prospective employer (someone to whom the applicant is applying for a job).

It is important to state facts, that is not to tell lies, and to give positive information.

An example of how you might set out your CV and the information you should include is shown on *page 27*.

You must take care with spelling, grammar and punctuation and, if you are not presenting a typewritten CV, you must make sure your writing is clear. It is best to use black ink because the CV may be photocopied by the employer and black ink copies more successfully than any other colour.

Divide the information into sections, each under separate headings. Some are a must, whilst others are only useful if they are relevant to you.

See the suggested headings and layout on *page 27*.

Sample layout for a CV

PERSONAL DETAILS

Name	*Include your full name(s).*
Address	*Ideally put each line of your address on a separate line. Don't forget your* **post code**.
Telephone no	*Include the area code if quoting a landline number.*
Date of birth/age	*Expressed as 8th March 1986 rather than 8/3/86.*
	Aged 20.
Nationality	*You might decide not to include this information.*

EDUCATION

Last school attended and qualifications gained	*1999 – 2004 (name of school)*	
	List only the Passes – be proud of your achievements.	
	2004 – GCSEs:	
	English Language	*Grade B*
	Mathematics	*Grade C*
	Key Skills:	
	Application of Number	*Level 2*
	Communication	*Level 2*
	ICT	*Level 1*
	etc., etc., etc.	
College attended and qualifications gained	*2004 – 2005 (name of college)*	
Non-academic achievements	*Passing your Driving Test*	
	Duke of Edinburgh Award	
	etc., etc.	
Work experience	*Name of firm(s), Dates, Job Title, Responsibilities*	
Leisure interests (hobbies)		
Referees	*Include two people's names and addresses if possible –* **however, check with them first that they agree to give you a reference**.	

Date (mm/yyyy). **You will need to know when your CV was written because you will be gaining additional qualifications and experience all the time and will want to update for most job applications.**

Covering letter to accompany a CV

Every time that you send out your CV you will need to send out a cover letter with it, whether you are sending your CV in response to an advertisement or direct to an employer.

A cover letter needs to say a lot more than just: 'Here is my CV!', which is all some people seem to think a cover letter should say.

It needs to tell the person why you are writing to them and outline why you are the ideal candidate for the job. You need to pick out the highlights from your CV that are relevant to the specific application, because most jobs you apply for will require a slightly different emphasis of your skills, qualifications and experience.

When employers receive hundreds of applications for one job it is important to get them to read and consider **your** CV. It is important to *show them you have style and are just what they are looking for*. A covering letter, clipped neatly to your CV, begins to get you noticed for the **right** reasons.

Points to remember

 Use good quality, plain A4 paper.

Use a fountain pen or a good quality ballpoint – it is acceptable to type your covering letter, but be sure, like on your CV, spelling, grammar and punctuation is 100% accurate.

Use black ink.

If handwriting, keep your lines straight – but do not use lined paper.

Use neat and legible handwriting.

Keep a copy of your CV and accompanying letter clipped together.

Use the correct name and address, and title of the person receiving the letter, if you know it.

Use a matching salutation and complimentary close.

There is an example of a covering letter on *page 29*.

12 Hospital Fields
York
YO1 5FW

18 June 2007

Miss M Stubbs
Personnel Manager
Fotherington and Crampton Store plc
2 Coppergate
YORK YO1 1FP

Dear Miss Stubbs

Your vacancy for a Junior Administrator

The Yorkshire Post 15 June 2007

I have read your advertisement for a Junior Administrator and I am keen to apply. Please find enclosed my CV with details of referees who have agreed they may be contacted on my behalf.

This would seem an ideal opportunity to combine my interest in computers and my interest in a retailing career, and I believe that I have the qualities and qualifications which your advertisement describes.

I am 17 years of age, I care about my appearance and I am enthusiastic and work well as a team member. Additionally, I have a computer and have done some introductory programming. I am ambitious and enjoy using my initiative and taking responsibility when given the opportunity.

I leave College on 23 June and I would be available to start work immediately afterwards. If you wish to interview me, I would be pleased to attend any day after 4pm or on a Saturday. After I leave College, I would be available for interview at any time.

I hope you will consider me as a candidate for the post.

Yours sincerely

Angelina Santos

Angelina Santos

Enc

INTERVIEW TIPS

Your job application form or your CV and covering letter impressed the prospective employer and you have been invited to attend an interview.

Study the following advice.

Arriving

Arrive early for your interview – to make sure you do this, carefully research public transport times/car parking arrangements. Know how long it will take you to walk to the employer's premises from the station, bus stop, car park, etc.

How to dress

Dress smartly and appropriately – forget about being the height of fashion for the day, and don't overload the jewellery.

Walking into the interview room

When called in to your interview, walk confidently into the room.

It is usual to shake hands with the interviewer(s). A firm handshake is important.

Be friendly

You should always maintain eye contact with the interviewer(s), especially with the person asking the question and with anyone to whom you are directing an answer.

Keep a friendly smile on your face to show your enthusiasm.

Sit up straight

Sit straight in the chair – don't slouch.

When you are nervous it is sometimes difficult to know what to do with your hands. When sitting, fold them on your lap and keep them still.

Speak clearly

Speak clearly and slowly. When you are nervous there is a tendency to rush your words. Slow down.

Avoid slang terms and poor grammar, such as "like", "basically", "actually", "absolutely", "er", "no problem", "obviously".

Listening to and answering questions

Concentrate carefully on the questions you are asked and so make sure you understand the question before you answer it.

If you don't fully understand a question, ask for it to be repeated.

Answer the question then stop talking. Don't go on and on and on with your answer.

You are allowed to think before you answer. However, don't spend too much time thinking.

Remember to direct your answer to the person who asked the question. If there are other people present, glance at them from time to include them in what you are saying.

Think in advance

If you have done your research into the job description and the company well, you should be able to anticipate some of the questions you will be asked. Prepare for these before your interview and know what you will say.

Promote your positive achievements

Be honest about your weaknesses but positive about your achievements and strengths.

At the end of the interview

Stand up and shake hands again, thanking the interviewer(s) for the time.

Walk confidently out of the room.

Some likely interview questions

Think about your responses to the following commonly asked interview questions:

- Tell me about yourself.

- What are your greatest strengths and weaknesses?

- Why do you want to work for us?

- What kind of salary are you looking for?

- What do you know about our company?

- Why should we employ you?

- Where do you see yourself in five years time?

- Do you mind working long hours?

- Tell me what you like best about your present job, and why.

- Tell me what you like least about your present job, and why.

- Tell me about when you have taken any responsibility.

- How do you feel about gaining further qualifications?

Would you like to ask any questions?

When the interviewer has asked all the questions she/he wishes, you are likely to be asked if you wish to ask any questions. Prepare a few questions in advance.

Of course, your questions depend on what was covered during the interview, but think about the following as possible questions:

- Are there opportunities for progression/promotion?

- Would it be possible for me to go to college to gain further qualifications?

- Would I be expected to wear a uniform?

- Would it be possible to see where I would be working?

Finally, you can ask those all-important questions:

- What is the holiday entitlement?

- What is the salary?

Don't ask the last two questions first – whilst you want to know these things, if the interview has not already given you this information, ask other questions first. You don't want the interviewer to think your only concerns are holidays and money!

COMMONLY MISSPELT WORDS

Word	word with different ending(s)
A	
A lot	
Absent	Absence
Absolute	Absolutely
Accident	Accidental
Accommodate	Accommodated
	Accommodating
	Accommodation
Accompany	Accompanied
	Accompanies
	Accompanying
Account	Accounting
	Accounted
	Accountable
Achieve	Achievement
	Achieving
Acknowledge	Acknowledging
	Acknowledgement
Across	
Activity	Activities
Address	Addresses
	Addressing
Advertise	Advertising
	Advertisement
Afraid	
After	Afterwards
Again	Against
Agree	Agreeing
	Agreement
	Agreeable
All right	
Already	
Altogether	
Amend	Amending
	Amendment
Amount	Amounting
	Amounted
Appear	Appearing
	Appearance
Article	
Attach	Attaching
	Attachment
Attention	
Avenue	
Awful	
Axis	Axes

Word	word with different ending(s)
B	
Bachelor	
Balance	Balancing
	Balanced
Bargain	Bargaining
	Bargained
Beauty	Beautiful
Before	
Begin	Beginner
	Beginning
Believe	Believer
	Believing
Benefit	Benefited
	Benefiting
Bicycle	
Borrow	Borrower
	Borrowing
Brake	Braking
Break	
Brilliant	Brilliantly
Build	Building
	Builder
Bulletin	
Burglar	Burglary
Business	
Buy	Buying
	Buyer
C	
Calendar	
Calm	Calming
Careful	Carefully
Carriage	
Catch	Catching
Category	Categories
Central	
Centre	Centred
Charge	Charging
Chief	Chiefly
Choose	Choosing
Chose	Chosen
Close	Closing
	Closure
Colleague	

Word	word with different ending(s)
College	
Compare	Comparison
	Comparatively
Competent	Competently
Complete	Completely
Compliment	Complimentary
Correspond	Corresponding
	Correspondence
Create	Creating
	Creation
Crescent	
D	
Data	
Decent	Decently
Decide	Deciding
	Decision
Defend	Defence
Definite	Definition
Delete	Deleted
	Deleting
Deliberate	Deliberately
Depend	Depending
	Dependable
Descend	Descending
	Descendant
Deserve	Deserved
	Deserving
Desperate	Desperately
	Desperation
Detached	
Develop	Developing
	Development
Dial	Dialled
	Dialing or Dialling
Diary	
Different	Differently
	Difference
Disappear	Disappearance
	Disappearing
Double	Doubled
	Doubling
Draw	Drawing
Drawer	
Duly	

32

Word	word with different ending(s)

E

Word	word with different ending(s)
Edge	Edging
Eight	Eighth
	Eighteen
Eighty	
Electric	Electricity
	Electrical
Elegant	Elegantly
	Elegance
Embarrass	Embarrassing
	Embarrassingly
	Embarrassment
Enter	Entering
	Entrance
Environment	Environmental
	Environmentally
	Environmentalist
Example	
Except	Exception
	Exceptionally
Excite	Excitement
	Exciting
Exercise	
Exhibition	
Expect	Expecting
	Expectation
Expense	Expensive
Experience	
Extreme	Extremely

F

Word	word with different ending(s)
Facility	
Fail	Failing
	Failure
Familiar	Familiarly
Favourite	Favourable
February	
Figure	Figuring
Final	Finally
Foreign	Foreigner
Fortune	Fortunate
	Fortunately
Forty	
Fourteen	
Friend	Friendly
	Friendliness
Fulfil	Fulfilment
	Fulfilling
Furniture	

G

Word	word with different ending(s)
Garage	
General	Generally
Gold	Golden
Govern	Governing
	Government
	Governor
Grammar	Grammatical
	Grammatically
Graph	
Guarantee	Guaranteeing
	Guarantor
Guard	Guarding

H

Word	word with different ending(s)
Half	Halve
Height	
Heir	Heirloom
Hero	Heroes
Humour	Humouring
	Humorous
	Humorously
Hungry	Hungrily
Hygiene	Hygienic
	Hygienically

I

Word	word with different ending(s)
Idea	
Identical	Identically
Immediate	Immediately
In between	
In fact	
In front	
Income	
Indeed	
Independent	Independently
	Independence
Innocent	Innocently
	Innocence
Insert	Inserting
	Insertion
Install	Installing
	Instalment
	Installation
Intelligent	Intelligence
	Intelligently
Intention	Intentional

Word	word with different ending(s)
Interest	Interesting
	Interested
Involve	Involving
	Involvement

J

Word	word with different ending(s)
Jealous	Jealously
Jewel	Jewels
	Jeweller
	Jewellery
Join	Joining
Journey	Journeying
Judge	Judging

K

Word	word with different ending(s)
Keen	Keenness
Keep	Keeper
	Keeping
Key	Keying
	Keyboard
Kind	Kindness
Kiosk	
Knife	Knives
Know	Knowing
	Knowledge
	Knowledgeable

L

Word	word with different ending(s)
Labour	Labouring
Laid	
Language	
Leave	Leaving
Legal	
Leisure	Leisurely
Library	Librarian
Lighten	Lightening
Like	Likely
	Liking
	Likelihood
	Likewise
Lonely	Loneliness
Loose	Loosely
	Loosen
Lose	Losing
Lovely	
Luxury	Luxurious

Word	word with different ending(s)

Word	word with different ending(s)

Word	word with different ending(s)

M

Word	word with different ending(s)
Magazine	
Main	Mainly
Maintain	Maintaining
	Maintenance
Manage	Managing
	Management
	Manageable
Marvel	Marvellous
Mathematics	Mathematician
Meant	
Menu	
Message	Messaging
	Messenger
Minute	
Mirror	Mirroring
Miscellaneous	
Month	Monthly
Most	Mostly
Move	Moving
	Movable
	Movement
Multiple	Multiply
My	Myself

N

Word	word with different ending(s)
Nature	Natural
Near	Nearly
	Nearby
Necessary	Necessarily
	Necessitate
	Necessity
Negative	Negatively
Negotiate	Negotiating
	Negotiation
Neighbour	Neighbourly
	Neighbourhood
Nerve	Nervous
	Nervously
New	Newly
	Newness
Ninth	
No one	
Noise	Noisily
Notice	Noticing
	Noticeable
Nowhere	

O

Word	word with different ending(s)
Object	Objecting
	Objection
Occasion	Occasional
	Occasionally
	Occasioned
Occupy	Occupying
	Occupier
Occur	Occurred
	Occurring
	Occurrence
Odour	Odourless
Offer	Offered
	Offering
Often	
Omit	Omitting
	Omission
Opinion	
Opportunity	Opportunities
Ordinary	Ordinarily
Original	Originally
	Originate
Owe	Owing

P

Word	word with different ending(s)
Particular	Particularly
Pay	Paying
	Payment
Perhaps	
Permanent	Permanently
Permit	Permitting
	Permissible
Persuade	Persuading
Phase	Phasing
Prejudice	Prejudicial
Prepare	Preparing
	Preparation
Present	Presence
Probable	Probably
	Probability
Procedure	
Profession	Professional
Prompt	Prompting
	Promptly
Proof	Prove
Public	Publicly
Punctuate	Punctuation
Pursue	Pursuing

Q

Word	word with different ending(s)
Qualify	Qualifying
Quality	
Quantity	
Quarter	Quarterly
	Quartering
	Quartered
Question	Questioned
	Questioning
	Questionable
Questionnaire	
Queue	Queuing
Quick	Quickly
Quiet	Quietly
Quite	
Quiz	
Quotation	

R

Word	word with different ending(s)
Rare	Rarely
Reach	Reaching
Ready	Readily
Real	Really
	Reality
Reason	Reasoning
	Reasonable
Receive	Receiving
Reception	
Recognise	Recognising
Recommend	Recommending
	Recommendation
Refer	Referred
	Referring
	Referral
Referee	Reference
Register	Registration
Repeat	Repeating
	Repetition
Reply	Replying
Responsible	Responsibility
	Responsibly
Restaurant	
Reverse	Reversing
	Reversible
Rough	Roughly
Route	Routing

Word	word with different ending(s)	Word	word with different ending(s)	Word	word with different ending(s)

S

Salary		Tend	Tendency	**W**	
Salutation		Ticket			
Scene	Scenery	Tomorrow		Waste	Wasteful
	Scenic	Tongue			Wastage
Secret	Secretly	True	Truly	Wednesday	
Secure	Securely	Truth	Truthful	Weird	
	Security		Truthfully	Whole	Wholly
Sentence		Try	Tries		Wholesome
Separate	Separately		Trying	Wield	Wielding
Sign	Signing	Twelfth		Wilful	Wilfully
	Signature	Type	Typical		Wilfulness
Similar	Similarly			Withhold	
	Similarity			Without	
Sincere	Sincerely	**U**		Wool	Woollen
	Sincerity				
Six	Sixth	Umbrella			
Speak	Speaking	Union		**Y**	
	Speech	Unnecessary	Unnecessarily		
Special	Speciality	Until		Yacht	Yachting
Success	Successful	Unusual	Unusually	Yesterday	
	Successfully	Use	Useful	Yield	Yielding
Surprise	Surprising			Your	Yourself
System	Systematic				Yourselves
	Systematically	**V**			

T

		Value	Valuable	
		Vary	Various	
Tariff			Varying	
Teach	Teacher		Variable	
	Teaching	Vegetable		
Temperature		Villain	Villainous	
Temporary	Temporarily	Virtual	Virtually	
Tempt	Tempting	Visible	Visibly	
			Visibility	
		Visible	Visibility	
		Volunteer	Volunteered	

COMMUNICATION: PART A, PRACTICE TASKS

TASK DESCRIPTION GRID

Number and title	Page	Activities	Refer to reference sheet(s) on page(s)
1 Hartburn Property Services	37	Completing an accident report from	6 – 7
2 Horse Racing	38	Working with a partner Designing a poster Designing a booking form	8 – 9
3 Poppy Garden Centre	40	Writing a fax	11 – 12
4 Sethcote	41	Reading a map Writing a personal letter	13 – 15
5 Binder and Page	42	Making a telephone call	10
6 Binder and Page	44	Writing a memo Drawing a graph	19 – 20 8
7 Rossetton	45	Drawing a map Reviewing your approach and outcome	
8 Dunn Cow Hotel	46	Writing a personal letter	13 – 15
9 Dunn Cow Hotel	47	Writing a business letter	16 – 18
10 Pets Safe at Home	48	Working with a partner Completing forms Writing a memo Reviewing approach and outcome	6 – 7 19 – 20
11 Hartley's Store	52	Writing business letters	16 – 18
12 With Us U R Safe	55	Writing a business letter	16 – 18
13 Friendly Faces	57	Writing a business letter	16 – 18
14 Heald Green Conference Centre	58	Taking part in a telephone call Writing a memorandum	10 19 – 20
15 Poppy Garden Centre	60	Completing telephone message sheets	21
16 Stop Smoking	61	Conducting research Designing a poster Working with a partner	8 – 9
17 First Steps to Fitness	64	Completing an application form	6 – 7
18 Planning a holiday	65	Conducting research Writing a report	23 – 25

TASK 1: HARTBURN PROPERTY SERVICES

Student Information
In this task, you will complete an **accident report form**, using information provided.

Ask your tutor for the blank **accident report form**.

REMEMBER:
Your form must be completed neatly and contain accurate and relevant information. Correct spelling and punctuation are important too.

See pages 6 – 7 for advice on Completing forms.

Study the report form carefully to make sure you complete all the relevant parts.

Completing an accident report form

Scenario
Today at your firm, **Hartburn Property Repairs and Restoration**, there was an accident on site.

You have to complete an **accident report form** with the relevant information supplied by the witness Terry Hughes (see his statement below).

Activities
Using the **accident report form** complete with the details as told to you by Terry Hughes.

Remember to include only relevant information and to word it appropriately.

Terry Hughes' Statement
"At 09:10 today, on the Blackmoor Site working on Unit 11, I saw Tom Higgins fall from the 7th rung of the 20ft ladder he had to climb to get to the roof he was repairing. He seemed to miss the 7th rung of the ladder.

Tom landed on the lawn and looked pretty bad at first. I called the First Aider – Mohsen Rowili – at 09:15 who suspected a broken arm. I then called the Site Doctor – Dr Stefan Marino – and he arrived at 09:25. He said he thought Tom had a broken arm and was not sure about his leg so an ambulance was called at 09:40 am.

The ambulance seemed to take for ever to arrive and at 10:15 they took him to Buxton General Hospital. He went to the A&E Department and was not admitted.

They diagnosed a broken arm and a sprained right ankle. It was his left arm that was broken.

He had his arm set and his ankle bandaged and was discharged from A&E at 14:15 pm. He went home and is expected to be off work for 6 – 8 weeks."

You look up Tom's address and find it is Flat 6, Blackbird House, Your Town BX9 3MN.

TASK 2: HORSE RACING

Student Information

In this task, you will work with a partner to design a poster, and on your own to design a booking form.

Ask your tutor for a blank copy of **Appendix 2 Pro Forma**.

REMEMBER:

Use the notes to design a poster.

Design the poster and include relevant image(s).

See page 8 – 9 on *Using images in communication.*

Ask your tutor if you can have a photocopy of the poster so that you each have a copy.

Design a booking form which includes all relevant information.

Make notes of the discussion you have with your partner.

Pay attention to spelling, grammar, punctuation and appearance of both documents.

Working with a partner to design a booking form

Scenario

Your firm is organising a trip for those employees who are interested in attending a horse racing meeting (at a track near your town) on the third Saturday of next month. You have to design an A4 poster to advertise this event to encourage employees to participate.

In order to keep track of bookings you have to design a suitable form.

Activities

You must complete the document, which is **Appendix 2**, to help you with your planning your work with your partner (for **Activity 1**).

1   Working with a partner and using the information contained in **Appendix 1**, design an A4-sized poster that, when complete will be printed and displayed on notice boards in the office.

      Make use of appropriate images and remember the purpose is to promote the event and encourage participation.

      If possible, photocopy the poster so you each have a copy of the evidence.

2   Working on your own design a booking form that will allow you to track which employees are taking part in the day out and if they have paid a deposit and the balance.

      Your form will need to record the name and extension number of those taking part.

      Don't forget to include an appropriate title.

Appendix 1

Details of the Horse Race day out on 3rd Saturday of next month.

Coach for 40 persons leaves the office on Saturday morning at 09:30 am.

Will return, leaving the track at 16:45 pm.

Reserved for the participants is the 'Hatfield Box' at the track and lunch will be in Box 7.

The races are as follows:

11:00	Jubilee Gallop
11:30	Ebor Hurdles
12:00	Top Hat Stakes
13:45	Golden Handicap
14:30	Jones' Builders Handicap
15:00	Philmore Stakes
15:30	Golden Anniversary Shield
16:15	Buckingham Hurdles

Buffet Lunch is 12:15 – 13:30 – price included in the cost of the ticket for the day £25

£2 deposit due by (next Friday). Remainder due the second Tuesday of next month.

You are in charge of the organisation and collection of monies (deposit and full amount), so you are to be contacted for further information etc. You extension number is 638.

TASK 3: POPPY GARDEN CENTRE

Student Information

In this task, you will write a fax message.

Ask your tutor for a blank **Poppy Garden Centre fax sheet**.

REMEMBER:

A fax is an official document, but it can be seen by anyone who comes across it on the fax machine before it is sent to the person to whom it is addressed. Be careful, therefore, not to be rude – just treat it like a letter that is delivered more quickly!

See pages 11 – 12 on Sending faxes.

Make sure that all the information you give is accurate and relevant.

Composing a fax message

Scenario

You work for **Poppy Garden Centre** and your boss – Petunia Flowers – has asked you to help her catch up with some outstanding work. The most important task she asks you to complete whilst she is out of the office, is to deal with an urgent order.

Activities

Read the handwritten note from Petunia (below) and compose the fax message to Roland Mole, using the fax paper provided.

Use the Fax Heading (Re)   Undelivered Order

There is 1 page

Tick   **URGENT** and   **PLEASE REPLY**

Remember to put Petunia's name at the end of the fax, although she will not sign it because she is not in the office.

Help:

Have just realised the monthly delivery (due 2 days ago) of top soil from John Mole and Co has not arrived.

We are desperate for this order and I am annoyed because I recall they delivered it 4 days late last month. We always PAY on time so it's not good enough. We've been dealing with them for 3 years now.

Fax them and request delivery tomorrow or we'll go elsewhere in future. If they don't deliver tomorrow - hard luck they've lost our business.

Ask them to confirm the delivery will take place tomorrow.

Pick the relevant bits out of that and fax them. Their number is 01649 6245 893.   Contact name is Roland Mole.

Thank you Petunia

TASK 4: SETHCOTE

Student Information

In this task, you will read a map.

You will then write a personal letter to a friend describing how to get to your home.

REMEMBER:

A personal letter is written from someone's home address to either an individual person (as in this task), or a company.

See pages 13 – 15 on *Writing and setting out personal letters*.

Spelling, grammar and punctuation are important.

Remember to sign the letter.

Giving directions from a map — writing a personal letter

Scenario

A friend is coming to visit you next month and you have to send her/him directions to your house. You live at No 3 The Glade in the village of Sethcote. Your friend will be driving and will come to the village along the main road, the A416, travelling southwards.

Activities

1   From the map shown in Appendix 1, plan how to write the directions to your home.

2   Write the directions in a personal letter to your friend. Make up a name and address for your friend. She/he is arriving on 5th, and leaving on the 9th.

MAP:

N

Sethcote : 3 The Glade

Manor House
St Edwin's Road
The Glade
Park Road
3
4
5
2
1
St Edwin's Park
St Edwin's Walk
Acorn Avenue
Cranberry Hotel
South Walk
Postgate Wynd
Front Street
Front Street
Curl Up & Dye Hairdressers
Tulip Grove
Library
St Edwin's Church
West End
The Golden Lion
Main Street
Lombard Avenue
PO
A416

TASK 5: BINDER AND PAGE

Student Information

In this task, you will read instructions then take part in a telephone call.

The purpose of the telephone call is to place an order for books.

REMEMBER:

Make notes, before your telephone call, of what you will say.

See pages 10 on Making telephone calls.

Make notes of what is said during the telephone call because you will use some of this information in **Task 6**.

You will need to introduce yourself and your company at the beginning of the call. Speak clearly and make sure you give accurate information.

End the call politely.

Making a telephone call

Scenario

You work in the offices of a booksellers – Binder and Page.

You have come into the office to read a message from your boss (Polly Page) asking you to make a call to order some goods.

You are to work with a partner to place the order. Your partner will take the role of working for Inky Characters.

Activities

1   Read **Appendix 1**.

2   With a partner taking the part of someone in Inky Characters, make the call and place the order detailed in **Appendix 2**.

Instructions for the telephone call to Inky Characters

- Introduce yourself and your company, making clear who you are.
- Be clear about why you are ringing.
- Give an order number.
- State the order, giving your partner time to repeat what you say.
- Make the delivery request.
- As you are making the call, you end the call. Think of what you could say.

Instructions for your partner working for Inky Characters

- Answer with the name of your company – you should give your name too.
- Make sure you get an order number.
- Repeat the order to check you have it correctly. Probably it would be best to do this after each item.
- Remind the customer that orders usually are delivered within 14 – 21 working days.
- You don't think it is possible to deliver within the week.
- Don't promise anything, but say you will try to deliver within 10 days from this telephone call. Don't be too difficult!

Appendix 1

I haven't had time to ring Inky Characters to place our weekly order.

Please phone through the order shown on the order form.

Be sure to ask for an URGENT delivery and establish WHEN we can expect the goods. We ideally want the books by the end of next week. Try to get them to deliver within a week if you can!

Good luck.

Thank you

Polly

Appendix 2

BINDER AND PAGE
17 Hallgarth Street
Your Town
DT7 1GK
Email: binderandpage@telemed.co.uk

ORDER

Order No: 5673/SS

Date: *Today's*

To: Inky Characters
The Print Works
Heathtown
HT3 9LS

Quantity	Description Book Title and Author	Catalogue No	Unit Price £
100	300 ways with Fish and Chips by Ivor Place	2679	5.99
20	Tree Planting for Beginners by Teresa Green	1165	6.90
30	Ice-Cream Making by Frosty Fingers	7450	3.99
50	Sheep Rearing Explained by Barbara Lamb	4440	15.00

TASK 6: BINDER AND PAGE

Student Information

In this task, you will use information from your telephone call in **Task 5** to include in a memo you will write.

You will also display information in a graph.

Ask your tutor for a blank **Binder and Page memo sheet.**

REMEMBER:

Your memo should be brief and you must sign it.

Be accurate with the information you include in your memo.

See pages 19 – 20 on *Writing and setting out memos.*

The purpose of an image, such as a graph, is to help the reader better understand the information.

Remember to give your graph a title and label and axes.

Writing a memo and drawing a graph

Scenario

You still work for Binder and Page and in the previous task you made a telephone call to **Inky Characters**, ordering some books.

Your boss – Polly Page – now needs to know the outcome of that telephone call, and has asked you to display details of book sales for last week in graphical form.

Activities

1   Using the memorandum paper, let Polly know the result of the telephone call to **Inky Characters**.

Address your memo to Polly Page and use the heading **Re Order Number 5673/SS Inky Characters**.

2   Display the following sales figures in graph form, using an appropriate graph title and using the relevant dates.

Book sales for the week Saturday to Friday (last week please):

Category	% sales
Sports and hobbies	25%
Computing	15%
Food and drink	5%
Cooking	30%
Fiction	25%

TASK 7: ROSSETTON

Student Information

In this task, you will work with a partner to draw a map that shows the route to your house.

You will also reflect on how you worked on this task and describe any difficulties you experienced. Ask your tutor for a blank copy of **Appendix 2 Pro Forma**.

REMEMBER:

You are creating an image and it should be clear and contain accurate information.

Read the instructions carefully before you start, and before each stage.

Drawing a map

Scenario

A pen friend is coming to visit you next week and you have to send her/him directions to your house.

Activities

1   Working with a partner, from the information contained in **Appendix 1**, draw the map to your home.

You will need to use one sheet of A4 paper and adopt a reasonably small scale so it fits comfortably on one sheet. Don't make it so small you cannot read it!

Be careful to label and name everything clearly.

2   Complete the form **Appendix 2 Pro Forma**, which will reflect your work in this task.

Appendix 1

Your friend is driving and needs directions to your village of **Rossetton**.

The following are the details for your map.

You friend will be driving on the **A818 road** (to the south of the map) and will take a **left turn** into your village.

Almost immediately after the turn into your village there is a **cross roads**. It is necessary for your friend to **turn right** into **Elm Lane**. The road straight ahead at the cross roads is called **Oak Chase.**

After she/he has turned into Elm Lane, there is a pub at the corner on the **left hand side of the road** called **The Green Dragon**.

Opposite the pub on the opposite side of Elm Lane is a building that is the **Library**.

Next to the Green Dragon Pub is the **Post Office**, which stands on the corner of a **left hand turn off into Conifer Way.**

Your friend has to turn left into Conifer Way.

The area to the right of Conifer Way is **St John's Park.**

There are two roads to the left off Conifer Way, the first is called **Poplar Grove** and the second, immediately after the first is **Ash Lane**.

Between Poplar Grove and Ash Lane, on Conifer Way, is **St John's Church**.

Conifer Way continues straight and there is a **right turn** off Conifer Way, immediately opposite Ash Lane into **Sycamore Close**.

There are 4 even-numbered houses on the right hand side, and 4 odd-numbered houses on the left hand side of Sycamore Close. The numbers begin 2 and 1 respectively as you enter Sycamore Close.

Your address is 5 Sycamore Close.

Mark your house.

Mark North on the map.

TASK 8: DUNN COW HOTEL

Student Information	REMEMBER:
In this task, you will write a personal letter to an hotel to book accommodation.	A personal letter is written from someone's home address to either an individual person, or a company (as in this task). *See pages 13 – 15* on *Writing and setting out personal letters.* Spelling, grammar and punctuation are important. Remember to sign the letter.

Writing a personal letter

Scenario
You wish to book a weekend break in a favourite hotel in Oxford.

Activities
Write a personal letter, using your own address and today's date, to Mrs P Holt, The Reservations Manager of Dunn Cow Hotel, Carlton Lane, Oxford OX3 6PK.

Ask the following:

● to reserve two single rooms and breakfast for the first Friday and Saturday nights of next month;

● the cost of bed and breakfast per night, per person; and

● if the hotel's fitness centre will be open during your visit and ask its opening times.

Say you will be arriving around 7pm on the Friday and request a written response confirming the reservation and your queries. The reservation is in your name.

TASK 9: DUNN COW HOTEL

Student Information

In this task, you will write a business letter from the hotel which features in Task 8. The purpose of the letter is to confirm the booking and give information.

Ask your tutor for a blank **Dunn Cow Hotel letter heading**.

REMEMBER:

A business letter is a formal document. *See pages 16 – 18 on Writing and setting out a business letters.*

See page 18, Useful phrases for business letters

Make sure it contains the following:

- The date it was written.
- The name and address of the person who will receive the letter.
- A salutation (Dear ?).
- A complimentary close that matches the salutation.
- The name of the person who wrote the letter.

Be sure to sign the letter.

Writing a business letter

Scenario

You are the Reservations Manager in the Dunn Cow Hotel, Oxford and have received the reservation request written for **Task 8**.

You now have to reply on the hotel's behalf.

Activities

Respond to the prospective guest as follows:

- Confirm the booking of two single rooms plus breakfast – the rate is £25.60 per person per night.

- The hotel's fitness centre will be open that weekend and its opening times are: **Weekdays 08:00 – 18:00, Saturdays 08:30 – 17:00 and Sundays 09:00 – 15:30**.

You may add any other information or comments that you think appropriate.

TASK 10: PETS SAFE AT HOME

Student Information

In this task, you will work with a partner to plan how you will complete the tasks. You will read a memo and from the information it contains, complete an **Assignment Register form** and a **Staff Assignment Details form**.

Ask your tutor for a blank **Pets Safe at Home Memo sheet**.

You will then write a memo to accompany the two forms you complete.

When the activities are complete comment on the advantages, or disadvantages, of working with a partner. Ask your tutor for a blank copy of the **Pro Forma** you will use for **Activities 1** and **4**.

REMEMBER:

You are expected to complete each form neatly and accurately. *See pages 6 – 7* on *Completing forms.*

Your memo is to Jennifer Black and do not forget to sign it.

See pages 19 – 20 on *Writing and setting out memos.*

Spelling, grammar and punctuation are important.

Your work must be laid out correctly and your meaning must be clear. Correct spelling and punctuation are important too.

Working with a partner and completing forms and writing a memo

Scenario

You work in the firm called **Pets Safe at Home** based in your city.

The firm offers a 'pet sitting' scheme for holiday makers, and as such, has a register of staff upon whom it can call, relating to their particular interest or specialist knowledge.

Your tasks today are to prepare lists for appointments for the month of May and you are required to work with a partner to each produce evidence for **Activities 1** and **2**. You are each required to complete your own forms, but your discussions should have helped you to get the information correct.

Activities

1   Complete **Part A** of the **Pro Forma** before you begin completing the forms and **Part B** after you complete the task.

2   Refer to **Appendix 1**. From the information it contains, complete the **Assignment Register – Appendix 2. (Appendix 2 has been partially completed for you)**.

3   After completing the **Assignment Register** complete the **Staff Assignment Details Appendix 3. This has been partially completed for you.**

Perhaps you will shade in the dates, but whichever method you use, make it clear which dates are involved.

4   On your own, send Jennifer a memo telling her you have completed the activities and are attaching the two forms you have completed.

Appendix 1

PETS SAFE AT HOME

M E M O R A N D U M

To   *Yourself*

From   Jennifer Black

Date   12 April 2007

Re   **Pet-sitting requests for the month of May**

The following requests have come into the office over the last three days.

Name	Type of Pet	Inclusive Dates
Mr and Mrs H Bird	2 cats and a tank of tropical fish	3 – 12 May
Miss T Prentice	3 hamsters	3 – 8 May
Mr C Jonty	Spiders (x3) and Snake	16 – 23 May
Miss G Walker	2 dogs and a rabbit	11 – 16 May
Mr and Mrs J Witherspoon	1 spider, 2 dogs and 2 mice	12 – 20 May
Miss S Putman	4 cats	22 – 29 May
Mr N Woods	Tank of tropical fish	15 – 22 May

Please would you complete the Assignment Register. Below are details of the staff I have allocated to each client.

Client	Employee
Mr and Mrs Bird	Philip Aynton
Miss Prentice	Sonya Jacobs
Mr Jonty	Martin Exelby
Miss Walker	Derek Sunley
Mr and Mrs Witherspoon	Stanley Acton
Miss Putman	Phillip Marks
Mr Woods	Joy Marton

Thank you

Appendix 2

PETS SAFE AT HOME

ASSIGNMENT REGISTER
For the month of May

Employee	Name of Client	Type of Pet(s) & Number	Inclusive Dates of Stay						
	Miss T Prentice								
	Mr and Mrs H Bird								
	Miss G Walker								
	Mr and Mrs J Witherspoon								
	Mr N Woods								
	Mr C Jonty								
	Miss S Putman								

Appendix 3

PETS SAFE AT HOME

STAFF ASSIGNMENT DETAILS MONTH OF ....

STAFF	CLIENT'S NAME	1	2	3	4	5	6	7	8	9	10	11	12	13	14	15	16	17	18	19	20	21	22	23	24	25	26	27	28	29	30	31
Sonya Jacobs																																	
Philip Aynton																																	
Derek Sunley																																	
Stanley Acton																																	
Joy Marton																																	
Martin Exelby																																	
Phillip Marks																																	

TASK 11: HARTLEY'S STORE

Student Information

In this task, you will write two business letters. The purpose of each letter is to apologise to the complaints made by the customer who has written a personal letter to the store.

Ask your tutor for a blank **Hartley's Department Store letter heading**.

REMEMBER:

A business letter is a formal document. *See pages 16 – 18* on *Writing and setting out business letters*, and *page 18* for some examples of useful business letter phrases you might want to include.

Make sure your letters contain the following:

● Date written.

● Name and address of the person who will receive the letter.

● A salutation and complimentary close that match.

● The name of the person who wrote the letter.

Be sure to sign the letters.

Spelling, grammar and punctuation are important.

Writing business letters

Scenario

You are the assistant to Sebastian Bregazzi, the Customer Services Manager in a department store called Hartley's Department Store.

Sebastian has received the letters in **Appendix 1** from two disgruntled customers and asked you to reply on his behalf.

Activities

1 **Letter from Mr Howlader**

Your first task is to apologise.

Then say the cooker is in stock and give him a choice of times when you will collect and deliver Monday and Friday afternoon or Wednesday morning.

In an effort to maintain good customer relations you are enclosing a cheque for £50 towards compensation for the inconvenience the customer has been caused.

2 **Letter from Miss Constance**

She is quite correct about all she says. Tell her the My Lady Petite Manageress – Janet Yarrow – is expecting Miss Constance to call on Saturday afternoon and will, indeed, refund the money she paid for the dress.

Apologise for the inconvenience and any embarrassment she may have been caused and enclose a £20 discount voucher that she can use in any of the store's departments.

Remember: you must adopt a tone and expression suitable for the situation and pay attention to spelling, grammar, punctuation and letter display.

Remember: the letters are written FROM Sebastian Bregazzi, Customer Services Manager.

Appendix 1

9 Haidene Court
Jasmine Road
Your Town
CF6 8BW

(dated yesterday)

The Customer Services Manager
Hartley's Store
Caledonian House
Pennypot Lane
Your Town
YT1 51K

Dear Sir or Madam

PORTILEX "SUPERCOOK 8" OVEN

The purpose of this letter is to complain about the above-named oven that I bought from your store on 7th of (last month).

When I took delivery of the oven it had a dented main oven door and the delivery man said he would report this and it would be replaced with an undamaged model. By 10th your store had not contacted me so I rang and spoke to Mr Simpkins (the Manager of the Household Department) who said he would order a new cooker, which would take five days to arrive in the store.

I still have not received the replacement and Mr Simpkins has not contacted me.

Please would you let me know when I can expect the replacement. I hope this is within the next seven days.

I look forward to hearing from you urgently.

Yours faithfully

H Howlader

H Howlader

Appendix 2

Swan's Nest
Pinders Brook, Your Town, CF4 2LS

(dated 3 days ago)

Store Manager
Hartley's Store
Caledonian House
Pennypot Lane
Your Town
YT1 5LK

Dear Sir or Madam

I wish to complain about a dress I bought from your My Lady Petite section. The dress cost me £139.50 in last month's sale. The first time I wore it, three evenings ago, about 40 cm of stitching came adrift on the left seam near the waist. Although I was unhappy about this, I wanted to wear the dress again yesterday evening, so I stitched the seam myself.

When I put the dress on yesterday, fortunately, before I left the house, almost the entire back seam became unstitched and the zip fell out.

I rang today and spoke to an assistant who said that I should return the dress and she would have it repaired for me.

I do not wish to have the dress repaired but want a refund of £139.50.

Please speak to the manager of the department and make sure that when I come into the store on Saturday afternoon, I receive £139.50 in cash.

Thank you for your co-operation.

Yours faithfully

Thelma Constance

Thelma Constance

TASK 12: WITH US U R SAFE

Student Information

In this task, you will write a business letter to reply to questions from a potential customer. The purpose of the letter is to encourage business.

Ask your tutor for a blank **With Us U R Safe letter headed paper**.

REMEMBER:

A business letter is a formal document. *See pages 16 – 18* on *Writing and setting out business letters*, and *page 18* for some examples of useful business letter phrases you might want to include.

Make sure your letter contains all the information necessary.

Spelling, grammar and punctuation are important.

Writing a business letter

Scenario

You work for the security firm **With Us U R Safe** and today have to reply to an incoming letter from a potential customer.

Activities

1   Read the incoming letter **Appendix 1**, together with the notes made by your boss (Mr Edmund Lever). Mr Lever is the company's Sales Director.

2   Compose a reply on behalf of Mr Lever, to Mr and Mrs King, using the letter headed paper provided.

Remember you must adopt a tone and expression suitable for the situation and pay attention to spelling, grammar, punctuation and letter display.

Appendix 1

FIR TREE COTTAGE
TULIP LANE
CHURCH WYCOME
BUCKS
WB5 6JJ

01864 745 6666
email: JKing@flowers.co.uk

(Dated 3 day's ago)

Mr E Lever
Sales Director
With Us U R Safe
18 Raffles Gardens
CHURCH WYCOME
Bucks
WB5 11FS

Dear Mr Lever

My wife and I moved into this bungalow six weeks ago. It has a burglar alarm installed but we would prefer to have this taken out and an up-to-date system installed.

We wonder if your company would be interested in coming to see our home and giving advice about the systems that would be suitable for the property?

We would be available at the beginning of next week on either a morning or an afternoon, so perhaps you would write and confirm your interest?

Yours sincerely

James King

James King

Please reply to the Kings.
Happy to visit and give advice.
Senior Installation Engineer,
Steven Hope, available next Tuesday
11 am, or Wednesday 2.30 pm.
Ask Mr King to telephone to
arrange an appointment at the most
convenient time for he and his wife.
Mr Hope will call, inspect the
existing system, then make his
recommendations.
Thank you   Edmund Lever

TASK 13: FRIENDLY FACES

Student Information	REMEMBER:
In this task, you will write a business letter complaining about services from a supplier. Ask your tutor for a blank **Friendly Faces letter heading**.	A business letter is a formal document. *See pages 16 – 18* on *Writing and setting out business letters*, and *page 18* for some examples of useful business phrases you might want to include. Make sure your letter contains all the information necessary and your tone is polite, but firm. Spelling, grammar and punctuation are important.

Writing a business letter

Scenario

You work in a residential home called **Friendly Faces**. The Manageress of the home is Kitty Barker.

Kitty is concerned about the non-delivery of fresh produce and has asked you to write to the supplier on her behalf.

The last four deliveries of fruit and vegetables from **The Farm Kitchen** have failed to be delivered on time. This is unacceptable.

When the Home placed the contract eight months ago it was on the understanding that deliveries would take place on Fridays and Tuesdays between 08:30 and 10:00am.

Activities

Kitty wants you to write, on her behalf, to the owner of the firm **Benjamin Spring** and complain. Kitty expects the agreed pattern to be re-established with next week's delivery and continue thereafter as agreed. If this is not the case, she will cancel the contract.

Write to: Mr Benjamin Spring, The Farm Kitchen, Your Town YT7 3PW.

Be firm, but polite. Use the letter heading provided.

Remember your tone should be appropriate to the context and you must pay attention to grammar, spelling and punctuation as well as the layout of the letter.

TASK 14: HEALD GREEN CONFERENCE CENTRE

Student Information	REMEMBER:
In this task, you will receive a telephone call then write a memorandum confirming details of the telephone conversation. Ask your tutor for a blank **Heald Green Conference Centre memo sheet** and a blank copy of the **Booking Checklist**.	You need to make notes of important points discussed in the telephone call. *See page 10 on Making telephone calls and page 21 on Taking messages.* The Booking Checklist could help you to remember, and record, important points. The memo should be written to Mr Seth Winters and contain relevant and accurate information. *See pages 19 and 20 on Writing and setting out memos.* Spelling, grammar and punctuation are important.

Receiving a telephone call and writing a memo

Scenario

You work as an Assistant Administrator in the **Heald Green Conference Centre** in your town. Your work today involves taking a telephone booking for the Centre.

Activities

1   You receive a telephone call (your tutor will take the part of the caller) from a prospective client wishing to book a conference room for the 25th of next month. You know you have the Emerald Room free on that date.

You will need **Appendix 1** in front of you when you take the call because you will be asked the cost of some facilities.

Deal with the caller and make any necessary notes because in **Activity 2** you will be writing a memo to your boss with details of the booking. At the end of the conversation ask for the caller to put their booking request in writing to your company. Don't forget to make a note of the caller's name and company.

> You might find it useful to complete the **Booking Checklist** as the call progresses so you have the information for **Activity 2**.

2   Write a memorandum to your boss – Seth Winters – confirming the booking you have just taken.

You will need to include:

●   Name and address of the company. Date of the booking and number of delegates.

●   Equipment required, refreshments and meals requested, with relevant times. Tell him you have asked the company to confirm the booking in writing.

Remember your memo must be laid out correctly and your meaning must be clear. Correct spelling and punctuation are important too.

Appendix 1

HEALD GREEN CONFERENCE CENTRE

Heald Green Your Town CH15 4BJ
01625 765377
healdcon@fsnet.co.uk

FACILITIES

Conference Rooms:

Topaz	Seating and tables for 125 people
Garnet	Seating and tables for 100 people
Amethyst	Seating and tables for 50 people
Emerald	Seating and tables for 25 people

All Conference Rooms have integral kitchen and dining area. Self-catering is available on request, otherwise the Centre's catering staff provide all food, drinks and refreshments to order.

Equipment available for hire:

Computers, projectors and screens	£12 per hour or part thereof
Video conferencing	£25 per hour or part thereof
Flip charts	£2.50 per hour or part thereof
OHP and screen	£4 per hour or part thereof
Photocopying facilities	5p per copy (black and white) 15p per copy (colour)
Fax	£5 per hour or part thereof
email	£20 per hour or part thereof
Internet	£20 per hour or part thereof

Rates

Topaz	£120 per day
Garnet	£100 per day
Amethyst	£75 per day
Emerald	£45 per day

Morning coffee and afternoon tea are included in the rate, together with a notepad, pen and pencil per delegate.

Lunch menus are available on request and prices start at £10 per delegate.

TASK 15: POPPY GARDEN CENTRE

<table>
<tr>
<td>

Student Information

In this task, you will complete two telephone message forms.

Ask your tutor to provide you with the blank **Telephone message forms**.

</td>
<td>

REMEMBER:

Telephone messages are brief.

See page 21 on *Taking messages.*

Telephone Messages contain only relevant information.

The information you include must be accurate.

Study the sheets carefully to make sure you complete all the important parts.

Spelling, grammar and punctuation are important.

</td>
</tr>
</table>

Completing telephone messages

Scenario

You work at **Poppy Garden Centre** and have had the following telephone conversations. You must now complete Telephone Message Forms.

Activities

In handwriting, taking special care of spelling and punctuation, complete the two forms with the details of the calls. These details can be found below.

In each case you enter your own name as having taken the message and the time is 14:10pm.

Note: a completed telephone message form contains only relevant information so you need to omit anything that is not necessary to the meaning of the message. Be careful to be accurate in what you write.

Message 1 – for Petunia Bloom, Centre Manager

Mrs Cynthia Paxton telephoned enquiring if we have in stock, or could get into stock, white agapanthus. She has recently returned from a holiday in Madeira and the hotel's garden had hundreds in flower. She has seen the blue ones in the UK, but never the white ones.

She can be contacted on 01865 562921 any day after 3.30pm.

If we can get these, or do have them, then she would like 20.

Message 2 – for Rose Bush, Equipment Department Manager

Colin Field, of Field and Meadow, telephoned today to say that our Order Number 348-33 has been processed and the goods will be leaving them tomorrow.

However, the Lawnspeed Supreme petrol mowers are not in stock with Field and Meadow and this item – we ordered 4 – has not been included in the consignment. Mr Field thinks these will be back in stock early next month and he will advise us when to expect delivery. He says he hopes we do not want to cancel the order.

If you want to speak to him about this, telephone on 01743 334 664 today, up to 3pm when he has to go out of the office. You can call his mobile after 4pm – 0784 736 991.

TASK 16: STOP SMOKING

Student Information

In this task, you will read information and use relevant parts of the information to design a poster to include relevant image(s).

You will then work with a partner to discuss your own and the other person's posters. You will write a summary of your discussion. Ask your tutor for a blank copy of **Appendix 3 Pro Forma**.

REMEMBER:

When using a image make sure it helps the reader to better understand the topic. Use an image to enhance and explain. *See pages 8 –9* on *Using images in communication.*

The information you include must be accurate.

Study the sheets carefully to make sure you complete all the important parts.

Spelling, grammar and punctuation are important.

Designing a poster and discussing it with a partner

Scenario

Your educational establishment is keen to promote **STOP SMOKING** to its students. The organisation already has a **NO SMOKING INSIDE** policy.

You have to design a poster on your own, then discuss it with a partner.

Activities

1   Using the information in **Appendices 1** and **2** design an A4-sized poster aimed at discouraging teenage smoking.

The Principal will look at all the posters produced and the one he thinks is the most successful in communicating the message, will be reproduced and displayed on notice boards around the building.

Make use of the information you have been given, and show you have understood the content of the graphs by including some of their information.

You should use appropriate images to help the reader understand some of the points you make.

2   When you have completed your poster, ask your tutor to select a partner with whom you can work.

With this partner you are going to discuss both posters and make recommendations for how to improve each of them.

Discussing your poster. You must tell your partner about your poster, i.e. why you included the information you used – why you thought it was relevant to the poster's intention; why you displayed the information as you did; why you chose the images it contains.

Your partner will listen, probably ask questions, and then you will discuss how your design could be improved.

After the discussion, make notes on the **Appendix 3 Pro Forma**.

Discussing your partner's poster. This time you will listen to your partner telling you about his/her poster and you will be the one to ask questions and offer suggestions for improvement.

Hand in your poster and the notes you made on the form in **Appendix 3**.

Appendix 1

Too Young to Die
Too Young to Buy

The Too Young to Die, Too Young to Buy scheme offers advice and support for retailers and can provide Retailer Packs, Window and Till Stickers and help with Age ID cards.

Around 450 young people start smoking every day.

80% of adult smokers start smoking during adolescence and continue into young adulthood.

50% of young adult smokers will still be smoking at 60 years old.

Smoking is a behaviour established in adolescence that for most will last for decades.

Nicotine Addiction in Young People

Teenagers have similar levels of addiction to adults – "once you have smoked four or more cigarettes, you are likely to become a regular smoker".

Symptoms of addiction can develop within weeks of the first cigarette.

Most adolescent daily smokers report symptoms of withdrawal.

Appendix 2

Smoking by age
(Prevalence of regular smoking by age)

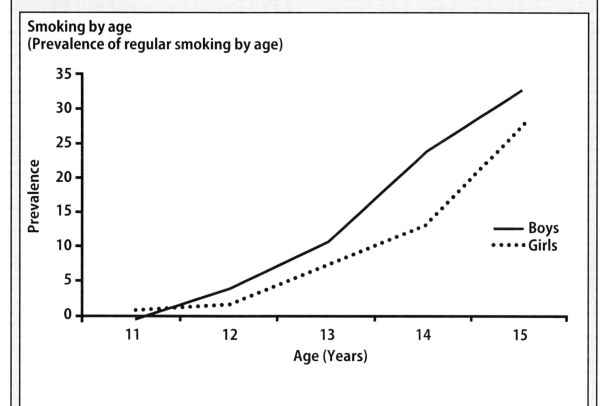

Trends in adolescent smoking
(Prevalence of regular smoking in 11 – 15 year olds)

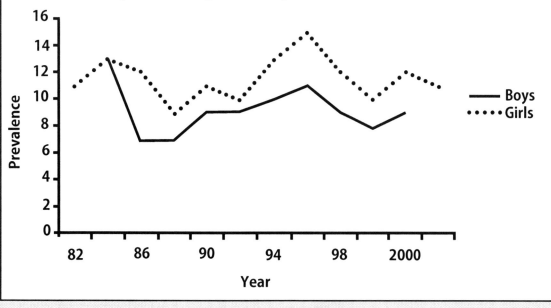

TASK 17: FIRST STEPS TO FITNESS

Student Information

In this task, you will read information and use relevant parts of the information to complete an **application form**.

Ask your tutor for a blank **First Steps To Fitness application form**.

REMEMBER:

Study the information carefully to make sure you complete all the important parts.

See *pages 6 and 7* on *Completing forms*.

The information you include must be accurate.

You are expected to complete the form neatly so it is legible.

Completing an application form

Scenario

It is your father's 40th birthday on 8th of next month and your family has decided to contribute towards getting him membership of the local health club – **First Steps to Fitness**.

It is your task to complete the **Application for Membership form**.

Activities

Complete the form, making up a name and address for your father.

His landline number is 01638 567822. Make up a mobile number and an email address.

You know this is an experiment so decide it will be best if he tries membership for 5 – 6 months. Select an appropriate Membership Plan. You think he is most likely to be interested in the Gym, and Steam Room and the Racquet Halls. Swimming is something he also likes, so be sure to select the option that will allow him to swim.

You want his membership to begin on his birthday.

Once the money has been collected by the family you will pay by cheque.

Sign the form in your name and date it.

Make sure you have completed the form correctly and that all relevant sections are addressed.

TASK 18: PLANNING A HOLIDAY

Student Information
In this task, you will find and read information based on the bullet points in **Activity 1**.

From the information you will write a report.

REMEMBER:
Include your research documents with the task you hand to your tutor.

If you cannot do this, take a photocopy of the documents you find, and attach the copy to the task.

Any images you use must be appropriate and help the reader to understand the topic.

See pages 23 – 25 for help on Writing reports.

Conducting research to plan a holiday within a budget and writing a report

Scenario
Yourself and two friends wish to have some sunshine so have decided to book a seven-day holiday somewhere in Europe. You have been given the task of conducting the research and informing them of your recommendations.

Activities

1   Conduct research into possible holidays taking the following into account:

- You each have a budget of £450 and can take your seven-day holiday at any time.

- You each have extra money to spend on entertainment and meals once at your resort – so the £450 relates to flights, accommodation and breakfast.

- You prefer to fly from an airport as close to your home as possible.

- You do not want a long journey from the airport to your resort.

- You want to go somewhere where there is a beach and sunshine.

- You would prefer a hotel near the beach.

- You want only bed and breakfast.

As a result of your research you will recommend **two** places for your friends' consideration (**Activity 2**).

You must provide evidence of your research and the notes you make from your documents.

2   Write a report (it is not required to be formal, but it must clearly state the purpose of your research, any criteria you had to take into consideration, your findings and your recommendations) from which your two friends can make a decision about which holiday to book.

Include any relevant images that will help the readers to understand what you write.

SAMPLE END ASSESSMENT

20 Multiple-choice questions

The following questions are multiple-choice. There is only one correct answer to each question.

Instructions

1   Choose whether you think the answer is A, B, C or D.

2   Ask your tutor for a copy of the answer grid (or download a copy from **www.lexden-publishing.co.uk/keyskills**).

3   Enter your answer on the marking grid at the end of the test.

4   Hand it to your tutor for marking.

A Communication Key Skills Level 1 External Assessment will consist of 40 questions and you will have **1 hour** to complete them.

How will you select your answers?

If you are sitting your End Assessment in paper format – not doing an online test – you will have to select one lettered answer for each numbered question. The answer sheet will be set in a similar way to the example below:

1   [a] [b] [c] [d]

2   [a] [b] [c] [d]

Make your choice by putting a **horizontal line** through the letter you think corresponds with the correct answer.

Use a pencil so you can alter your answer if you wish and take an eraser to allow you to change your mind about a response. Use an **HB pencil**, which is easier to erase. (If you make two responses for any one question, the question will be electronically marked as **incorrect.**)

Take a **black pen** into the exam room because you will have to sign the answer sheet.

Your tutor has a 100 sample End Assessment questions and you will be given these when your tutor considers you are ready to practise the questions.

QUESTIONS

	Line
PROBLEM FOR "AURORA"	
The P&O cruise liner company launched a new, luxury passenger cruise ship in 2004 – Aurora. Her first major voyage should have been a round-the-world cruise lasting 109 days beginning 9th January 2005.	
Unfortunately, this luxury cruise ran into stormy waters in, surprisingly, the English Channel and more than 1,700 paying passengers had an exciting time in the port of Southampton only.	Line 5
The ship suffered problems with its propulsion system and the passengers were entertained by some TV stars and offered free food and alcohol if they chose to stay aboard to wait for the ship to set sail after the repairs.	
After repairs, the Aurora undertook a test run to Torquay and back, after which passengers were told they would finally set sail that afternoon, nine days late and that the shortened cruise would last only 98 days.	Line 10
The £106 million 76,000-tonne German-built ship entered service originally in 2000, before her 2004 refit. It seemed as if there were bad omens and that she was jinxed from the start. During her naming ceremony, the bottle of champagne swung at her by the Princess Royal fell harmlessly into the water without breaking. The ship broke down in the Bay of Biscay on her maiden voyage, costing its owners £6 million in compensation. Following this she was hit by a virus outbreak in 2002. The virus returned in 2004, when 600 passengers and crew fell ill.	Line 15

Questions 1 – 7 relate to the text Problems for "Aurora", above.

1 The cruise has been reduced by how many days?

- A   5
- B   15
- C   90
- D   11

2 The word "jinxed" appears on Line 13. Which alternative word could be used without altering the meaning?

- A   fortunate
- B   unlucky
- C   trouble-free
- D   famous

3 How has the shipping company been trying to keep the passengers happy whilst the ship is in port in Southampton?

- A   Providing free meals.
- B   Providing free alcohol.
- C   Providing free meal, alcohol and entertainment by TV stars.
- D   Providing entertainment by TV stars.

4 Where was the ship built?

- A   Southampton
- B   Bay of Biscay
- C   Gibraltar
- D   Germany

5 Which of these words could **best** replace the word "**omens**" that appears in Line 13?

- A   indication
- B   warning
- C   signs
- D   feelings

6 What happened to the ship on her maiden voyage?

- A   The crew became ill.
- B   She broke down.
- C   The passengers became ill
- D   The champagne bottle did not break

7 According to the text, which of the following statements is true?

- A   The grand voyage set off from Southampton on 9th January.
- B   The first virus attack was in 2004.
- C   The ship cost £106 million and was built in Southampton.
- D   Major technical problems will again cost the owners, P&O, many millions of pounds in compensation

67

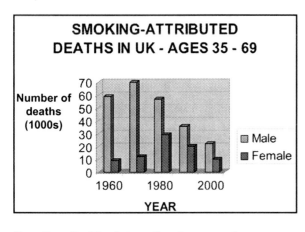

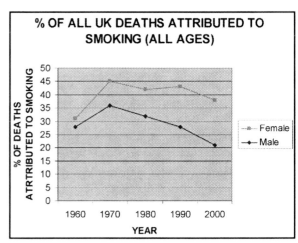

Questions 8 – 10 relate to the above graph.

8   Looking at the chart above, which of the following statement is true?

   A   The greatest number of deaths from smoking took place in 1980.

   B   The number of deaths from smoking is evenly split between male and female.

   C   In 1970 the greatest number of females died as a result of smoking.

   D   A greater number of males die from smoking-attributed diseases.

9   In which year was there the fewest smoking-attributed deaths of females?

   A   2000

   B   1990

   C   1970

   D   1960

10   In which year was there the greatest smoking-attributed deaths of males?

   A   1990

   B   1970

   C   1960

   D   2000

Questions 11 – 13 relate to the above graph.

11   Which year saw the lowest percentage of male deaths attributed to smoking?

   A   1960

   B   1980

   C   2000

   D   1990

12   Which year saw the highest percentage of male deaths attributed to smoking?

   A   1970

   B   1980

   C   2000

   D   1990

13   Looking at the graph above, which of the following statement is true?

   A   There has been a steady increase in the percentage of male deaths.

   B   There has been a steady increase in the number of female deaths.

   C   There has been a steady fall of male and female deaths.

   D   After an initial increase, male deaths have fallen, whilst female deaths have shown a steady increase.

UK WEATHER FORECAST						
	Mon	**Tues**	**Wed**	**Thur**	**Fri**	**Sat**
London	10	15	12	13	13	14
Aberdeen	10	8	11	10	11	11
Belfast	8	13	8	13	12	12
Birmingham	10	14	9	13	12	12
Glasgow	10	11	13	13	12	14
Cardiff	12	15	14	14	14	15
Leeds	9	12	11	11	10	10
Manchester	9	13	11	13	13	13
Newcastle	11	9	10	10	10	10
Oxford	10	14	11	13	12	13
Plymouth	13	14	17	12	12	12

Questions 14 – 18 relate to the above table.

14 Looking at the table above, if the cities were arranged in alphabetical order, which cities would be out of place?

A London and Newcastle

B London and Cardiff

C Cardiff and Glasgow

D London and Glasgow

15 Which city can expect the highest temperature on Friday?

A London

B Cardiff

C Glasgow

D Newcastle

16 Which city can expect the lowest temperature on Monday?

A Belfast

B Plymouth

C Leeds

D Manchester

17 What is the highest temperature forecast for any city in the 6 days?

A 15

B 17

C 18

D 13

18 What would be a **better** title for the document?

A British Weather Forecast

B Six-Day City Forecast

C The Changeable British Weather in April

D The Week Ahead

19 In which of the following sentences are the apostrophes used correctly?

A The ladies' club was holding a meeting and the chairs had to be brought out of the cupboard.

B The ladies club was holding a meeting and the chairs' had to be bought out of the cupboard.

C The lady's club was holding a meeting and the chair's had to be brought out of the cupboard.

D The ladies' club was holding a meeting and the chairs' had to be brought out of the cupboard.

20 Which of the following sentences does not contain any spelling or grammatical errors?

A It was a difficult busness to run but it was, at the moment, sucessful.

B It was a difuccult busines to run but it was, at the moment, successful.

C It was a difficult business to run but it was, at the moment, successfull.

D It was a difficult business to run but it was, at the moment, successful.

INDEX

Also from Lexden Publishing:

Title	Author	ISBN
Computer Systems Architecture	R Newman, E Gaura, D Hibbs	978-1-903337-07-0
Computer Networks (2nd Edition)	P Irving	978-1904995-08-X
Databases	R Warrender	978-1-903337-08-0
Get On Up With Java	R Picking	978-1904995-18-0
JavaScript: Creating Dynamic Web Pages	E Gandy, S Stobart	978-1904995-07-4
Multimedia Computing	D Cunliffe, G Elliott	978-1904995-05-0
User Interface Design	J Le Peuple, R Scane	978-1-903337-19-6
Visual Programming	D Leigh	978-1-903337-11-0
Website Management	G Elliott	978-1904995-21-0
Access 2002: An Advanced Course for Students	S Coles, J Rowley	978-1904995-06-7
Access 2000: An Introductory Course for Students	S Coles, J Rowley	978-1-903300-14-5
Access 2000: An Advanced Course for Students	S Coles, J Rowley	978-1-903300-15-2
Excel 2002: An Advanced Course for Students	J Muir	978-1-84445-005-3
Excel 2000: An Introductory Course for Students	J Muir	978-1-903300-16-9
Excel 2000: An Advanced Course for Students	J Muir	978-1-903300-17-6
Word 2000: An Introductory Course for Students	S Coles, J Rowley	978-1-903300-18-3
Word 2000: An Advanced Course for Students	S Coles, J Rowley	978-1-903300-19-0
The Small Book of Big Presentation Skills	R. K. Bali, A. Dwivedi	978-1-904995-17-3
Key Skills Level 1: Information and Communication Technology	R Whitley Willis, M Kench	978-1-904995-27-2
Key Skills Level 2: Information and Communication Technology	R Whitley Willis, M Kench	978-1-904995-26-5
Key Skills Level 2: Communication Technology	R Whitley Willis	978-1904995-31-9
Key Skills Level 1: Communication; Application of Number; Information and Communication Technology	R Whitley Willis, L Gabrielle	978-1904995-10-1
Key Skills Level 2: Communication; Application of Number; Information and Communication Technology	R Whitley Willis, L Gabrielle	978-1904995-17-9

To order, please call our order hotline on 01202 712909 or visit our website at **www.lexden-publishing.co.uk** for further information.

Printed in the United Kingdom by
Lightning Source UK Ltd., Milton Keynes
138010UK00001B/116/A